Purposed to *Live*

Anthony Ray Gambrell

ISBN: 978-1-952511-04-2

Editor: Sharp Editorial, LLC

Publisher: Chynna Creative Co.

DEDICATION

This book is dedicated to my wonderful parents, Annette Mildred Gambrell and Derrick Edward Williams. May they continue to rest in peace as their legacy lives on. The impact of their love helped me hold on to my life. Their lives were examples of how to make life count. Though our time was cut short, I appreciate knowing our relationship was on great terms when they left this earth. I will love and cherish them forever.

TABLE OF CONTENTS

ACKNOWLEDGMENTS

In life, we often hear that it takes a village to raise a child. I would be remiss if I didn't take the time to recognize and give thanks to my village:

To the medical staff, doctors, nurses, speech therapists, physical therapists, occupational therapists, church leaders, intercessors, friends, and family – *Thank you doesn't suffice.*

To my brothers of Phi Beta Sigma Fraternity Inc. and my sisters of Zeta Phi Beta Sorority Inc. – *I appreciate you.*

To the ones who visited, called, and sent texts; to my classmates who checked on me and sent gifts – *Thank you x1000000.*

To two of my heartbeats, my niece, Tiana Odell Jones, and my nephew, Dorian Rashaun Gambrell – *I love you dearly!*

To my sisters and brothers, especially my sister, Latonya Tashelia Gambrell – *Your love, support, strength, and love during my time of need means the world to me. Thank you for everything! You didn't miss a beat. What our mom was unable to do, you were right there to see this thing through with me.*

Thank you, everybody, for every ounce of love, seed, support, prayers, and concern.

INTRODUCTION

"Our will to live is often much greater than the difficulties of life."

Mehmet Murat Ildan

It was November of 2018, and I had just returned home to Charleston, South Carolina, from New York, to switch my summer clothes for winter clothes. I had plans to be at home for four days and then head back to New York for work. After saying a temporary "goodbye" to clothes that reflected the memories of my

1

amazing summer, I headed to a friend's house for a catch-up session. From the moment I walked in their door, we laughed and caught up on one another's life – you know, work, relationships, and everything in between. A few minutes into our reunion, I had excused myself to the restroom. At that moment, I noticed something suddenly felt different. I was enveloped by numbness, as though my body was covered in the numbing gel from the dentist's office. Shrugging off this foreign feeling, I proceeded to flush the toilet and wash my hands. As I washed my hands, I took a glimpse in the mirror and realized my face did not look the same on both sides. My reflection looked like something from a distorted mirror at a funhouse. Horror was slowing sinking in, yet I continued to examine myself as I tried to piece together some sort of explanation for these random, sudden changes. I was able to wink with my right eye but not my left. Then, I tried to smile, and only the right side of my mouth formed a curve. At that moment, I knew I was having a stroke. Within seconds of my realization, I tried to yell for help, but I couldn't form the words.

I was terrified.

Honestly, "terrified" is putting it mildly.

I was afraid for my life.

"There is no way my life is ending right now," I thought in fear as I contemplated the worst.

Thoughts of my mom's sudden passing came to mind, and I began imagining the worst for my life. My mind went from thoughts about my mom to thoughts of never speaking again. The simple phrases I used to speak that I once took for granted became words I wished I could shout, let alone say.

Hello.

Can anybody help me?

Can you hear me?

Yet I couldn't manage to mutter a mere syllable.

Then, the image of my mom's final moments crossed my mind, and I wondered if my bathroom crisis mirrored her last breaths on Earth. The physical and emotional pains from that moment in the bathroom were excruciating.

As badly as I wanted to continue attempting to cry out for help, my tongue was slightly twisted, and the only noises I could manage to make were inaudible groans. Worse, my friend's house was in the country, and the nearest hospital was 20 minutes away. I knew every second mattered, and I needed medical attention immediately.

Some may wonder how I was able to maintain a sense of logic during this frightening ordeal. Truth be told, I wonder the same, but in retrospect, I realize that my experience in the airline industry and as a licensed massage therapist had trained me to detect and react logically to various signs and symptoms of medical emergencies. I never thought I would be on the other end of an emergency, yet this was one of those moments when my training kicked in, thank God, and I was able to respond accordingly.

That afternoon, I knew I didn't have time to wait for an ambulance. Every second mattered. So, I bolted from the bathroom, grabbed my car keys off the kitchen counter, and left my friend's house. Not only could I not wait on an ambulance, but I also couldn't wait for my friend to figure out the reason behind my sense of urgency, and because I couldn't speak, I knew there was no use in playing charades.

"Be safe!" my friend confusedly shouted, seemingly stunned and caught off guard by my sense of urgency. "Call me," he pleaded.

I nodded my head, hopped in my car, broke every speed limit, and rushed to the emergency room. I was in fight-or-flight mode, and I never thought about the chances of having another stroke or losing control of my vehicle, which are quite common in my situation. My only focus was darting to the hospital and figuring out the rest later if God was willing to grant me a "later."

Thankfully, He granted me time and safety during that trip to the emergency room.

When I got to the hospital, I ran inside and tried to explain to the staff at the front desk that I was having a stroke. Leaning over the nurse's station, I grabbed my chest and whispered in the nurse's ear, "I'm having a stroke," as I stuttered and struggled to articulate. The nurse immediately hopped from her seat, placed me in a wheelchair, and rushed me to the back of the hospital as other nurses began running blood work and other tests on my body. Strangely, despite the chaos, my mind was able to re-focus on the fact that my car was a rental, so I started anxiously wondering how I would return the car on time. My health was ever-present in my mind, yet I was panicking about everything else going on, big and small.

Come to find out, my blood pressure was 220/180. I had congestive heart failure and fluid on my lungs. The staff tried to determine the cause of these issues, but the facility was rather small and didn't have the equipment to treat or diagnose me properly. Although the doctor reviewed my symptoms and confirmed I experienced a mild stroke, he felt the need to reach out to a neurologist who was able to assess and confirm that I did, in fact, have a stroke. The staff prepared me for transport to another hospital, about 40 minutes away, which was equipped to deal with my condition.

Overwhelmed with emotions I had never felt until that moment, I started to cry. Tears were flowing, and it seemed as though they'd never stop.

"I did this," I remember murmuring. "I messed up my life. This is my fault," I had cried, no longer able to silently contain the pain, sadness, and regret of ignoring my symptoms in the past.

Despite my anger, I felt a slight sense of relief, knowing I was transitioning to a facility that could properly treat me, yet that feeling of gratitude quickly escaped my mind because I suddenly remembered I did not have medical insurance. I felt overwhelming regret from opting out of medical insurance at work, and I felt like a child as I received lecture after lecture from the hospital staff, and deservedly so, for getting behind the wheel and driving to the hospital. They were in sheer disbelief that I put myself and others in danger by driving minutes after having a stroke.

When the staffers left my room, I called my sister, who lives in upstate South Carolina. I was hesitant to call, but I knew I needed her to know what was going on, in the event anything was to happen to me – anything as in death. I knew questions were bound to come but I also knew I didn't have the answers to all of them. Unlike my usual prepared self, I was only in the position to murmur "I don't know" or "I'll have to find out for you," and I hoped that would suffice for my sister, although I knew it wouldn't.

My sister is a nurse, so her medical background made the conversation slightly better than I feared, but my real concern was that her mind would go to Mom, and I didn't want my sister to fear that this was the end for me, too.

***

I've always had a strong will to live. In fact, I've fought for most of my life because I deeply wanted to live a life of uncompromised joy, but that fight came equipped with many roadblocks. For years, I battled feelings of depression, namely for situations that transpired in my life, especially rejection. Without giving a great deal of attention to matters I've worked through and healed from, I once battled with feelings of rejection because I did not know my biological father until I was 13 years old. Some events, including the question mark over my father's life and identity, caused me to want to throw in the towel. Admittedly, I tried several different ways to take my life. I had once felt that my will to leave was greater than my will to live.

Years ago, however, I finally found a place of peace and happiness, a place where I no longer allowed certain situations and people to have power and control over my life. This was no easy feat, and as many know, those who have fought for their peace, there comes a time when you feel enough is enough, and nothing is worth your joy. In my case, I knew I wanted to keep my sanity intact, and I was willing to do whatever it took. I came to this realization after my mom passed, and during this challenging time, I felt the power of God stronger than ever. I felt Him urge me to trust Him more and rely less on man and myself, too. As I gained peace, a peace that could only come from Him, I felt more confident in myself and my

11

decisions. I also learned that we always have a choice. We can choose to let the weight of the world drag us down and overtake our lives, or we can choose otherwise. We don't have to settle for defeat, and so, I chose not to settle. In refusing to settle, I found a place of peace.

This place felt great.

This place felt free.

Finally, I felt capable of pressing on rather than looking towards giving up, but on November 8, 2019, this place of peace, joy, and happiness became comprised. The life I had fought so hard to live was now coming to take me away, or so I thought.

I found myself in a position I had never been in before. I heard all the stories but never thought, not even for a second, that this could be me, fighting for my life as a young man with many more years ahead. During life-altering events, I've heard people say they've seen the light at the end of the tunnel as if their life flashed before their eyes. I've heard people say they experienced an out-of-body experience, able to see themselves on the outside of their situations, yet none of this happened to me.

There I was, in a dreary, desolate, and cold hospital room, attached to several machines. Cords were everywhere – I had a heart monitor, IV fluids, a blood pressure machine, and a saline solution treatment, which helped reduce my risk of a second stroke. As I tried to get up to use the restroom, everything suddenly turned pitch black.

"What's happening?! Did life just stop for me?" I wondered in sheer panic as I tried to gain my footing and piece together what was going on around me.

I couldn't see anything but darkness, yet there wasn't a tunnel that people speak of and no light in sight. I was alive but indescribably confused.

"Was this death?" I quietly wondered as I tried to navigate through the darkness that enveloped my body.

I felt confused. I had no idea what in the world was going on, whether I was living or descending. There wasn't a solitary moment when my life flashed before my eyes. I saw no one, dead or alive. No music was playing, certainly no beautiful harp and no singing choir. There were no flames beneath me, no angels in my vicinity, or anything else for that matter. All I had were my thoughts, and I couldn't help but think this was the end. Not only had my sight vanished, but my ability to hear was gone, too. I was petrified and confused, yet among the confusion and fear, I heard an inner voice, a voice urging, "Anthony, go back."

Then, I had an "ah-ha" moment,

believing I was in an in-between state of life and death. I felt as though I was physically present to the outside world, but my spirit and mind were in a realm on the outside, not necessarily Heaven or hell, just somewhere between life and death. Assumedly, this was the unknown, frightening space where people remain until they ascend or descend.

As I came to this realization, I immediately refused for this to be the end of me. I refused to let go. I refused to go out like that, to give up without a fight. My sight was gone, and my hearing was out of commission, too, but I felt the breath in my lungs, and that was all I needed to know that I was still here, still present on Earth. I tossed my fear to the side and decided to fight. I didn't know what this fight would look like or entail, but I knew I was going to hang on and somehow make my way through this.

"This is *not* the place I want to be," I decided, and that was the only definitive thought on my mind.

A few moments later, as my nerves calmed a bit, I reminded myself of the life I wanted to continue living.

"I have things to do!" I thought. "I have loved ones to see. I want to see more of the world, and I have a life waiting for me on the other side of the unknown."

It seemed I was in this meditative state for hours, but only a few minutes had passed, probably the longest couple of minutes of my life. Thanks to the visitor in my room, he began to explain I had a second stroke just a few minutes ago. I couldn't help but wonder if I was dreaming. I remained unsure. I tried to scream, yell, and call for help, but nothing came out. At that point, I could only assume I had died. For the life of me, I couldn't decipher whether I was dreaming or dead. As I quieted the unnerving thoughts in my mind, my inner voice spoke again. "Anthony, go back!"

Accepting this call on my life, I began to cry out for help again. This time, I was able to let out a whisper, although it certainly felt like I was shouting at the top of my lungs. I was able to open my eyes, only to discover the room was spinning, and I had double vision. My mind was intact, but my body had completely fallen apart. However, I knew life was waiting for me, a life I valued to have, a life I was determined to live. Looking back, I'm amazed that I managed to plant a mustard seed of faith and let it grow into a feeling so powerful that it propelled me not to give up, not even in my darkest hour.

Who knows what would've happened if I let my negative thoughts take control of me?

What I do know is that I experienced a

terrifyingly defining moment, a moment that I pray you never have to face.

As I share my journey with you, I hope you find the will, determination, and perseverance to fight for your life, and not just from a physical standpoint but mentally and emotionally, too. Everyone has some sort of life plan, whether it's completely mapped out or just a few ideas stored inside, but please know there will be detours and curveballs along the way. Those are inevitable. After all, life isn't perfect, and no matter how much we plan, we can't control fate. However, when obstacles arise, you can choose to accept defeat or face those challenges head-on and aim to *win*.

You see, when you have a will to live, a will to survive, a will to improve, and a will to thrive, the enemy will do any and everything to extinguish your flame and increase your odds of accepting and succumbing to failure.

My story is that of defying the odds and coming out on top, a journey that may seem unbelievable, but one that reminds you that we serve an incredible God, a God whose plans are greater than ours could ever be. With God at my side, I put up a fight against death, a battle I was never supposed to be a contender in, and I came out victorious. I wasn't fighting His Will. I was fighting the enemy's plan to cut my life short.

I am a survivor, a warrior, a fighter, and a miracle.

I am victorious!

Life may present you with challenges, but through each encounter, you have the power and strength, physically and mentally, to conquer your greatest fears and biggest obstacles.

This is my story, and I welcome you to

read it as I recall a time that still feels unreal to this day.

CHAPTER ONE

"Therefore we do not lose heart. Though outwardly we are wasting away, yet inwardly we are being renewed day by day. For our light and momentary troubles are achieving for us an eternal glory that far outweighs them all. So we fix our eyes not on what is seen, but on what is unseen, since what is seen is temporary, but what is unseen is eternal."

2 Corinthians 4:16-18

As I laid in my hospital bed that day, the day I had a series of strokes, I felt hopeless and confused. So many questions ran through my mind. It was as if my mind couldn't be at peace or quiet itself for a minute. With each question that crossed my mind, I felt worse about my condition and the unknown.

How is this going to end?

Is this the end?

Am I doomed to live a life dependent on others helping me?

I couldn't imagine a life where I needed people to help me do everyday things, everyday things I realized I once took for granted. Whether needing a sip of water or wanting to change the television channel, I wondered if I would always need assistance. I prayed I wouldn't, but I had no idea what to expect. One would think I had all the answers to the questions plaguing my mind, seeing that I was at the hospital, but if anything, I only had more doubts and confusion.

At the time, I underwent a great deal of testing, so doctors could detect any blood clots that may have caused my stroke. They needed to stabilize my body by giving me saline through an IV. The doctors ran several tests on me, from CAT scans to endoscopes to MRIs and countless blood tests, but nothing was detected, not a single clot or abnormality. Upon receiving the results of these tests, my doctors grew increasingly concerned because they wanted to prevent future strokes, but they were unsure how to proceed, considering these tests left them no room to come to a conclusion, let alone speculate. If they had found something, at least I could have peace of mind and a plan moving forward, but since nothing turned up, an indescribable fear factor kicked in, and I began to wonder if I would have to be monitored forever.

I also started to process feelings of stupidity, as I felt horribly foolish for not paying attention to the warning signs.

Before starting my recent job, I was working three jobs to make ends meet, and let's just say they never met. At the time, I had recently moved back to Charleston after the company I was working for was in the process of selling their business. This had left me with a decision – stay where I was and find something different or go back home and rebuild my life. I was at a place in my life where I wanted to travel and enjoy the world, but my pockets said otherwise. So, I decided to go home, rebuild my life, and work somewhere new.

When I returned to Charleston, I started practicing massage therapy again at a local spa. I was also trying to find a part-time bartending job, but this proved to be a challenge because jobs in this field were scarce. However, I finally lucked up and obtained a part-time bartending gig at a hotel. My work schedule was full, but I was grateful to make a good living. Then, I added one more job to my plate, as I began working at the airport, part-time, in ground transportation and at the ticket counter.

Although each job was great, they weren't what I wanted in life. Yes, I was elated to be home, but I wanted more. I desired to travel and to make money somehow.

So, I put in the work to take my life to new heights. From practicing my interview skills, researching various airlines, and studying for pertinent tests, I prepared to pursue a competitive field and drawn-out process. The time, effort, and work to get into this career made it more rewarding to be chosen out of thousands who were also vying for coveted wings. Coming into my career, I had financial challenges I was still working to overcome, and I recognized it would be even tougher for me the first few years, as I was trying to solidify a stable life.

When one starts in the airline industry, the money hardly flows in. So, I needed to see where I could make cuts in my life. Because of my ongoing travel schedule, I did not need a car or car insurance, which helped tremendously, but I still needed to make a few more sacrifices. I monitored my spending in terms of dining out and needs versus wants, but the truth is, I was in survival mode. To this day, sharing that truth sends a chill down my spine because I pray no one must choose between quality health care and basic life necessities, but that's the harsh reality of countless American citizens. Everyone isn't afforded healthcare, and many of us are forced to choose. In my case, I chose to deal with the consequences because health insurance was going to cost me more than I was willing to come out of my check each month to pay. Sadly, I made countless cutbacks, yet I was still broke. I stretched my food to the last day possible and reverted to the days of being without, surviving off .10 cent packs of noodles, grits, and water. Several coworkers knew my struggles of starting in the industry, and they helped me in so many ways, never wanting or expecting anything in return. Those special people knew the importance of paying it forward, and I vowed to do the same when I eventually moved out of this trying time.

I had decided against purchasing insurance so that I would have disposable income and not be completely broke. This decision wasn't the smartest idea by far, but I felt it was necessary at that time. I figured I could pay for minor doctor appointments out of pocket, and that would be that. I felt safe in knowing I wasn't having any medical issues or so I thought. Nevertheless, I began working and experiencing a whole new life for myself.

My financial woes were real, yet I was living my dream, tightly holding on to the fact that this financial hardship would pass. From the early stages of my career, I was able to care for and assist people, something I always wanted to do through professional endeavors. Monetary challenges aside, I reached a place in life that felt good. I mean, it felt great. My life was coming together for the better, and that was largely in part due to my position of helping others. I was a small-town young man, experiencing the world in ways I never imagined while caring for people in the process. This was winning. This was winning on my terms, and I was doing it.

However, my body was going through a lot more than I realized. I was having problems breathing while sleeping. From 3 am to 6 am, I felt as if I was in and out of death. During those hours, my chest felt restricted, and the ups and downs of my breathing were unbearable, but I would wait until it passed because I figured my issue was due to sleep apnea. Basically, I completely ignored the fact that this issue could've been something worse. I assumed this was a painful side effect or product of sleep apnea, never thinking that this issue could be the beginning of the end.

At the time, I worked different shifts – overnight, over 12 hours at a time, and early in the morning – and I believed my sleeping issues and chest pains were a part of dealing with a hectic schedule. I didn't go to the doctor because I had chosen against an insurance plan, and I didn't want to go into crazy debt. Yet again, I figured I would be okay and that everything would work out, so I didn't see the value in going to the doctor.

Two months before my first stroke, I remember there was one day when I was off work and having a good time with one of my roommates in New York. Thanks to the reserve stage of my job when I essentially worked on-call, I was afforded opportunities to meet with loved ones and spend my time off with them. During this get-together, we were laughing and having a good ol' time, but then the strangest thing happened. I got up to throw something away, and out of nowhere, I was on the floor. Apparently, I blacked out, hit my head on the wall, and was out cold. None of this made sense since I was just standing and feeling fine, or so I thought I was fine. This should've been the moment I knew something wasn't right, but I ignored it and went about my life, maybe because I regained consciousness shortly after that. I chalked it up to exhaustion. Nonetheless, I made an excuse for what should've been a major red flag.

CHAPTER TWO

*"The point is you have family and friends who love
you. You have a world out there just waiting for you to
conquer it. You have a life that will be anything you
make it. That's the point."*

Malorie Blackman

Although I knew a stroke was serious,
something inside of me refused to believe my
situation was that bad. Part of me convinced
myself I would be out of the hospital within a
matter of hours. Silly, I know, but I was in

denial. I started thinking I was merely there for observation, yet every medical staffer that entered my room reiterated the seriousness of my condition. There I was, unable to move or feel the left side of my face, yet I had the audacity to convince myself that my status was not that serious.

Maybe this was my way of coping with the situation.

Maybe I needed to find a way to make myself feel better and not become depressed.

Maybe I channeled my fear into a new avenue of denial, and that seemed to suit me just fine at the time.

That false sense of denial was short-lived because four days later, while I remained in the hospital, I experienced a second stroke, which landed me in ICU. Yet again, I was at a total loss of words. Despite the chaos and unknown, my doctors gently let me know I needed to rest and focus on getting better. That was easy for them to say, but "relaxing" was a foreign concept for me at that moment. My world had stopped, but everything around me was still trucking. My bills remained, my job was expecting me to show up, and other responsibilities awaited. I knew I needed to contact my job to let them know. The planner in me was going insane because this was throwing a total loop into my life. Imagine trying to focus on your wellness yet having to quiet the thoughts in your mind about your finances, relationships, and above all else, your life.

While in ICU, three different doctors checked on me daily. Thankfully, I was among medical professionals with incredibly pleasant bedside manners. They were increasing my saline intake to keep me from having another stroke. They wanted to keep personal visits limited and demanded me to rest. In fact, they wanted me to stop using my phone so that I would focus only on relaxation.

During this time, my immediate family, fraternity brothers, sorority sisters, close friends, and people I used to sing with in ministry came to visit me. Before the doctors' request to put my phone away, I shared my health status via social media. I felt the need to share something about my condition, as I could imagine the worry my loved ones felt when I suddenly went ghost on platforms. Since I was only able to verbally communicate above a whisper, which was hardly effective because my tone was slow and slurred, my sister allowed me to give others her number so that she could share further information.

Despite my sister's willingness to communicate with anyone who had questions, I had nothing set up to where anyone would be able to access the things I needed to handle, financially speaking. I knew I needed to communicate with my job and all my bill collectors. So, I tried my best to do this on the low but seemed to get caught by the nurses. Plus, my inaudible voice made it rather difficult to communicate effectively. I was met with several statements and questions such as "can you repeat that" and "I can't hear you." My sister quickly caught on to my need for assistance, and she played a major part in helping me handle things.

From communicating with doctors, being my point of contact in my personal life, and remaining by my side whenever she had a second away from work, my sister's role was monumental in my quest for healing. Plus, she works in the medical field, so having her nearby to ask the pertinent questions plaguing my mind was a relief.

I knew that seeing me in this state was causing my loved ones to be concerned. The thoughts of my parents passing away and having heart complications and hearing that my issues were hereditary didn't sit well with me or anyone else for that matter. It was even worse for my loved ones to hear those truths. I didn't want to think the worst was happening, but I couldn't help it.

There was a medical professional on-site and her job was to make sure I was cared for and resting. She would come in every day and talk so low as if we were in a library. She would whisper things like, "Are you getting enough rest?" I would always tell her what was going on and how I was feeling. One day, she came by, and one of my loved ones had stopped by my room. I was in and out of sleep, but I remember hearing the information shared regarding my situation, and all I heard was, "do whatever you need to do to save his life." Hearing this brought tears to my eyes. I knew my family and friends were concerned, but at that moment, those words gave me another reason to fight.

I needed help to do basic things. However, I refused to accept that helplessness would be part of my permanent life. I felt increasingly angry that this medical professional wanted me to be isolated from the world. I wanted to feel normal. I wanted some sense of normalcy when everything around me felt foreign and unfamiliar, which meant accessing my phone and having a connection to life outside my challenging reality. This woman was doing her job, and I certainly respected her, but the disconnection aspect was emotionally brutal.

My stay in the ICU broke me down yet challenged me in so many ways. Before my stroke, I never had major health issues. I was an independent man with a great deal of energy and enthusiasm for life, even in my day-to-day tasks, yet there I was, dependent on others for everything. I had to have nurses feed and bathe me. I would receive a daily sponge bath. I wasn't even able to use the restroom on my own, and it was awful. Instead, I received a rollaway toilet, which they needed to help me use. My independence was taken from me, and I had to humble myself to be helped. Nevertheless, the staff treated me with the utmost respect and gave me loving care. Having no short-term memory, no ability to walk, unable to talk effectively, or any coordination skills, I laid in bed with few abilities. Plus, the right side of my body was not functioning. Imagine having laryngitis, fighting to get a few words out, yet held back from doing so because of the strain on your voice.

That was how I felt as I attempted to communicate. Not being able to get up and walk around on my own was terrible. I felt helpless and experienced a mind-blowing glimpse of a physically bound life.

As time passed, doctors started to see an improvement. The swelling on my brain had reduced tremendously and my blood pressure decreased and was reading normal. From a physical standpoint, my face was no longer as droopy around the mouth and eyes. Regarding communication, my tongue had become more relaxed, and my words weren't as slurred and strained. So, they decided to release me from ICU, but I was going to need a lot of therapy to fully recover.

CHAPTER THREE

"You may not control all the events that happen to you, but you can decide not to be reduced by them."

Maya Angelou

Upon my release from ICU, I was placed in a hospital room on a regular floor. I was able to lift my right arm but unable to place my finger on my nose. Those sorts of movements and coordination had not returned. Although I was able to raise my arm, I could not hold it up very long. Those brief tests were clear indications I needed to remain in the hospital and receive ongoing care.

Although the plan was to walk the long road ahead and attempt to recover, I wanted to get back to work.

"Anthony, you won't be able to work in your career field again," my doctor had said. He was certainly not rude in his approach, but I understood he needed to be direct regarding my condition. "The average person recovers within one to three years, and most people remain immobile in some form or fashion," he continued to explain.

I heard what he said, but I refused to believe I would be "immobile."

Immobile.

That word rang in my head like a screeching freight train.

There I was, without insurance, and my doctors were explaining that I needed to undergo rehabilitation to walk, talk, write, and regain my memory and coordination. Meanwhile, I couldn't do anything but lay in bed. To get to the restroom, I needed nurses' assistance. I experienced constant pain in my ankle from not being able to move around freely. Also, my speech was awful. I talked like I was whispering, and my words remained severely slurred. This became a challenge for me because I was used to talking quickly. My mind went faster than the words were able to come out. I wanted to laugh aloud again. I wanted to express myself. I wanted to sincerely share an "I love you" with my sister and the other people who stuck by my side during my lengthy hospital stay. I wanted to show emotion, the same emotions I took for granted before my stroke. Most of all, I wanted to sing. Singing has always been part of my life. Whether an old-school R&B song or a hit tune on the radio, I loved belting out the words to a beautiful song. As a young boy, I used to go into the bathroom, lock the door, and play music to sing along to – Dru Hill, Jodeci, Luther, Xscape, and the incomparable Mrs. Whitney Houston – I used to sing their songs out and feel so free with each note.

More importantly, I wanted to worship His name through song. I wanted to give Him the praise He deserves and loves to hear. Personal moments of worship and singing along to Yolanda Adams, Kirk Franklin, Mary Mary, Fred Hammond, Hezekiah Walker, John P. Kee, and the other Christian greats were something I deeply missed. Pastor Donnie McClurkin, one of my all-time favorite inspirational leaders, was one I missed singing along to, and I wanted more than anything to return to this place of normalcy. I was no longer able to have those intimate moments of worship, and I felt the essence of my being shrinking a bit each day.

Within 24 hours, after being placed on the regular floor, I was able to start feeding myself, but it remained a slow process. I would take so long to finish one dish, but I wanted to do this to be free enough to handle everyday tasks on my own. This simple task required a great deal of focus. I needed to force my hand to gather the food and then place the food in my mouth. I can't help but laugh when I think about how quickly I used to eat, especially before a shift at work. At this point, I prayed for the spoon to graze my mouth. Nevertheless, I knew that eating on my own was one step closer to executing other independent acts.

Two steps forward and a few steps back, as my lack of insurance crept up again. The issue came back as to how I was going to pay for rehab. I had no idea where the money would come from, but I knew something needed to work out to get me to a better state of well-being. I needed to be able to stand up and take a shower without assistance, brush my teeth without missing my mouth, and do the everyday tasks I once took for granted.

The hospital certainly cared about saving lives, and the staff was nothing short of incredible. However, they also needed to establish an understanding as to where the money would come from for these treatments. Understandably, they are a business, and these questions need to be asked and answered. There was one doctor who showed an outpouring of care and attention regarding my condition.

"No matter the cost, I will see to it that you get better," he had said one afternoon.

Those words were extremely comforting, and I knew I was in good hands.

Rehab was at the forefront of my mind, and as my in-patient experience continued, doctors informed me I would be placed on a strict diet to help me lose weight and control my blood pressure. I was well over 300 pounds and carried most of my weight in my upper body, which caused more pressure on my chest, making my heart work harder. The doctors told me I would have to go on a low-sodium to no-sodium diet. I would have to stop eating beef, pork, and sweets and stop drinking sodas (which I wasn't drinking for a long time anyway). I also couldn't eat potatoes (except sweet potatoes) and no green leafy vegetables (which was due to one of the medications they assigned me to take). If I chose to eat or drink those items, I could bleed out and die. This meant no fried foods, no bread, no pasta, no sugar (only sweeteners and honey), and no alcohol. I could eat baked items such as chicken, fish, turkey, nuts, fruits, and other vegetables that weren't leafy greens or potatoes. I was permitted to drink water and unsweetened tea with sweeteners. As a total foodie, this was awful to hear because I wondered how I would happily live without pork belly, ribs, the occasional prime rib, and sweets. Yes, sweets! I was the type of person that would eat sweets before eating a real meal.

"You mean to tell me no more red velvet cake, Debbie cakes, sugar cookies, and cheesecake?" I questioned. "How am I supposed to eat on this restricted diet but can't have any lettuce to make a salad?" I continued, believing that this was crazy.

Coumadin, also known as Warfarin, was one of my medicines that helped reduce blood clots. While taking Warfarin, I was to stay away from leafy vegetables because they have high amounts of vitamin K. I was told that vitamin K needed to be controlled because I could bleed out or develop more blood clots. That meant no collard greens and sautéed spinach. If I was to eat those foods, I was only allowed to eat five ounces at the same time every day. This was virtually impossible.

Yes, I wanted to do everything in my power to change my diet and save my life, but at the same time, everything was changing, and these changes were hard to digest, literally and figuratively. I knew I'd give it my all, but my mind needed to adjust to these drastic changes. So, I did what was asked and began eating the hospital food within my dietary restrictions. Although I was to start this journey immediately, I wanted one last meal. You know, a meal to indulge. I wanted BBQ pork ribs, homemade mac and cheese, and some cake. Although I didn't get that exact meal, one of my family members agreed to bring me something yummy. I enjoyed a Chic-Fil-A sandwich with cheese, and it was everything, despite not having permission to eat it. At that moment, I realized it's entirely possible to eat hospital food, hate it, yet feel immense gratitude for being alive. Those random happy hour drinks I once enjoyed, sipping a cold drink after a long day of work, were no longer in the cards. I already longed for the occasional margarita, chips, and queso, and simple life pleasures I began to see as major fortunes.

About two days later, my doctors informed me that I was ready to start the rehab process. This was music to my ears, but my inner symphony was halted by the fact that my insurance was putting the brakes on my progression.

A woman from the financial office of the hospital came to speak with me about my plans moving forward. She wanted to see if I would qualify for any type of assistance to receive rehab treatment. If I weren't to qualify for in-house treatment, I would have to do out-patient rehab, which I would have to attend three times per week. Outpatient rehab wasn't an option for me since I wasn't able to drive, and I couldn't have the people around me completely re-work their schedules within their already busy lives. So, I knew that wasn't the route I wanted to go. She came back the next day and let me now that they had processed my application, I would be placed in their in-house rehab program, and I would receive a 100% charitable contribution for this treatment.

My rehab was going to be completely covered by charity, and to this day, I get goosebumps as I recall that life-changing news.

The tears began to flow as I couldn't feel anymore thankful for this news. I was going to be moved to the rehab floor and receive help, in-house, from all the staff. After a few more days in a regular room, I was relocated to the hospital's rehabilitation center and started working with a physical therapist, speech therapist, and occupational therapist to begin my road to recovery.

CHAPTER FOUR

"Pain doesn't last. And when it's gone, we have something to show for it. Growth."
Kamal Ravikant

Rehab had officially begun. I viewed this as the start of the work needed to rebuild my life. Every day, I had sessions with each of my therapists, and the nursing staff would periodically check on me. At each change of shift, the outgoing lead nurse would say goodbye, and the oncoming nurse would introduce themselves.

My days would start with getting up around six in the morning. At this point, I was finally able to move around with the assistance of a walker. Every morning, one therapist would come to my room and help me prepare for the day. They would help me get my clothes together and get ready. I wanted to get back into a normal routine, so at this point, I refused for help with bathing. I would tell them I need to use the restroom, and then I would take a shower on my own. They knew I was trying to operate on my own, and instead of holding me back, the staff was extremely supportive. They were concerned about the effort I was exerting yet applauded my determination and didn't try to discourage my attempts.

The toilet had rails to assist with getting up and down. The shower had a bench, so I was able to sit down and wash or take a break when tired. I was up, and though I couldn't move quickly, I was jumping for joy inside like a kid excited for the first day of school. I was about to begin the journey to become whole again. The thought of my former life outweighed the anxiety of how much work it was going to take to regain my well-being. I wanted nothing more than to be normal again, and normal remained the goal at hand!

As I was getting ready, I had to leave the door cracked, just in case the therapist needed to come in and help me. I also refused to continue having people help me get dressed, brush my teeth, and wipe my bottom. I was going to do all that myself, no matter what. So, I would get dressed, brush my teeth, and brush my hair to the best of my abilities, which looked a mess at the time, but I was doing it on my own and that's what mattered, yet I couldn't help but think I looked awful. These were major milestones, but when I looked in the mirror, I saw an unkempt man. I needed to shave, and I desperately needed a haircut. I don't care what people think and have never been concerned about the opinion of others, but I was always raised never to do certain things. My grandmother would always tell me not to leave the house looking "any old kind of way." "Don't go to bed wearing dirty underwear," she would say, and I would laugh a bit until she explained that one never knows if they will need help during an emergency, and the last thing you want is to be "dirty and nasty."

Growing up, my mother worked nights, so my aunt and grandmother stepped up to raise my sister and me. My aunt's love for me was beautifully expressed throughout my life. She was the epitome of a second mother –

loving, wise, and patient. My grandmother was my rock and always kept it real with me, whether I was right or wrong. Our relationship was that of an open-door policy. We talked about almost everything, and I miss her dearly.

As I continued to challenge myself in these everyday tasks, the only pain I experienced was in my right leg. My ankle and toes felt like I had a Charlie horse that wouldn't move or go away. The doctors determined this feeling was from laying in the bed for almost two weeks.

After getting ready for the day, the time came to eat breakfast. The hospital staff brought my breakfast around seven, and after breakfast, I was to go to my first therapy session of the day. Each day in therapy was different. I received my schedule the evening before to let me know what was happening the next day, which helped me mentally prepare for the day ahead. Each evening, I went to bed, determined to reach the goal intended for the following day.

When I got to the therapy room, there were all sorts of equipment to help with the process. This facility was state-of-the-art with top-of-the-line equipment. During my first session, the goal was to get out of the wheelchair and work on my balance. I remember the feeling of being so weak as I attempted to sit up and down. I would use the handles for help, but I had no strength to get up at a reasonable pace. Working on the balance part, though, was terrifying!

I was to try and stand without support, close my eyes, and remain still. To not move from side to side or fall required a great deal of focus. At that time, I was able to move my legs but unable to walk. Although I couldn't walk, I saw this as a process rather than a failure or hindrance because when I initially entered the hospital, I couldn't move my legs at all.

"Little by little," I would tell myself.

To stand up with no support was a huge feat. I would stand in one place, close my eyes, take one foot off the ground, and hold steady. When I tell you panic shot through my body, that's putting it mildly. I panicked.

What if I can't do this?

What if I fall?

What if I can't stay still?

Those thoughts plagued my mind, and anger began to rise within, too. Standing was something I used to do without thinking, yet there I was, unable to do a standard movement I mastered at one year old. I hated this feeling and process, but I refused not to try. Like a baby learning their first steps, I figured if I fell a few times, so be it. I needed to relearn to walk.

During my first attempt, I began to lift one leg with my eyes closed, and it happened – I fell – but the therapist caught me, thank God. So, I tried again. This time, I wanted not to fall. I braced myself and began to lift my leg slowly. I suddenly felt myself losing my balance but was able to regain it. At that moment, I was like a baby flamingo learning how to stand on one leg. For a few seconds, I was able to keep still, but those few seconds were all I needed to increase my confidence and push me to continue trying.

During each session, we continued to work on those goals, and each physical therapy session was meant to help me regain my everyday ability to do normal activities. I would do activities such as trying to get up and hold on to the railing in the hallway in an attempt to walk. Walking was scary because of the risk of falling. It was challenging because I still felt a deep pain in my right side. This pain was very uncomfortable, so the staff started giving me aspirin to try to reduce the aches, but it was a temporary fix. I tried my best to walk and not put pressure on that side, but it was challenging because I needed to learn how to walk properly and not just awkwardly shift my weight. So, I started dragging my leg and not bending it, yet the pain wasn't giving up, and neither was I. For several days, I remained in a wheelchair and learned how to maneuver with my chair.

Each day, physical therapy brought new challenges. I found myself being short of breath and not being able to stand for long periods. I would have to stop and take several breaks before proceeding. A few days had gone by, which meant new goals were in the works, one I was dreading.

One day, I faced a long walkway with two rails on the side, and in the middle of it stood a balancing ball. This wasn't an ordinary balancing ball. This ball was different because the top was a flat disc. It reminded me of one of my favorite childhood toys – Skip-It. However, I wasn't about to have a good time showing off Skip-It skills and hopping down the street. This was about me trying to walk down this aisle to the balancing ball and holding myself steady. The fear that came over me had me so shook up, but my therapist reassured me I would be okay and that she was with me. Her words were supposed to be comforting, but I found no peace in them. All I knew was I hadn't taken my feet completely off the ground at this point, yet I was required to do that and keep myself balanced. I just couldn't see that happening. My confidence was growing, sure, but I was also realistic, and this goal seemed out of reach.

I started to walk down the aisle as the therapist remained behind me, prepared to catch me if I fell. To get a feel for walking this aisle, she had allowed me to use the rails and walk down without getting on the ball. I did that with no problem. On the way back, she asked me to try it without using support

"Okay, let's see how this goes," I said, attempting to exhale the anxiousness from my body. I figured, if anything, my therapist was right there to catch me. Then again, I looked at her tiny frame and wondered if she could catch my body. I was well over 300 pounds, and if I fell, I would crush her. She sensed my apprehension and asked another therapist to assist. Knowing two people were nearby gave me comfort.

I began to walk with no support from the rails. Then, I reached the middle of the aisle and was instructed to stop and step on the ball.

This was the part I was dreading! Nevertheless, I went for it. I got up on the ball but hesitated to close my eyes and let go of the rail. I was only one foot off the ground, but you would've thought I was on top of a skyscraper looking over the ledge. This shook me to my core because I have a terrible phobia of heights. As I looked up in sheer panic, I saw something that completely restored my faith. Our Father always seems to give something to reassure us of His Word and motivate us to get to our step, whatever that step may be.

In the physical therapy room, several people were working to meet a goal. In front of me stood two therapists and a woman they were working with, a woman who appeared to be worse off than me. Seeing her made me stop and remind myself that I have more mobility than others, and I should be grateful. I have no idea what happened to the lady in front of me and why she was there, but they had her strapped into a harness hanging from the ceiling with a brace supporting her upper body. In order to walk, she needed to be supported by this harness.

When I saw her attempt to walk, I lost it. My emotional state was already all over the place, but this took me somewhere, and I needed a moment to gather myself. I asked the therapist to please let me have a second so that I could take in what I saw. I didn't share with them what was going on, but I let them know I needed a moment to gather my emotions. They were okay with this, so I stepped down from the ball and began to weep. My journey was trying yet at that moment, God reminded me that I'm further along than I realized.

CHAPTER FIVE

"Inspiration may come from many places but motivation — the love of life, daily drive, and the will to thrive — that must come from you from within."
Rasheed Ogunlaru

Being in the hospital, having to deal with the reality of my speech and writing skills not being what they used to be, was an emotional and physical struggle. Holding a simple conversation or writing down a few thoughts here and there, things I did every day for years on end, were now a struggle, and I desperately wanted normalcy in my life. I'm not big on talking, but I would take a long, drawn-out conversation over not being able to speak freely. From jotting down a few to-do list items to penning my feelings to simply wanting to ask a question about my treatment plan, I struggled to communicate, and these struggles added to my emotional battle.

At this point, my speech remained impaired. I still was unable to speak at a normal rate, which was a hard truth to grasp, seeing that I talk fast naturally. I had to learn how to communicate by talking slower and making sure I was over pronouncing my words. This took a lot of concentration. I needed to thoughtfully and purposefully push out each word and every syllable. Working with my speech therapist, she would take me through exercises that helped me regain my ability to talk. Most of the time, my sessions with her were in my room. Some days, she would wheel me outside, and we would have sessions on the patio. Despite the challenge of learning to speak at a normal pace, being outside felt wonderful. I felt so free – to see the cars, feel the wind, and see all the people walk in and around the hospital – and I realized I had missed the feeling of being one with nature.

By this time, I had been stuck inside this hospital for almost two weeks, so all I knew was the hospital bed and walls, and though I had lots of friends and family visit and around-the-clock care from the hospital staff, I was over being confound to this type of restricted living. I'm a free spirit by nature, so having to be restricted in my everyday life was a challenging concept to accept. I was used to going where I wanted when I wanted, even if that meant a quick walk outside. The outside has always been a place of peace for me, especially the beach. I love feeling the breeze from the ocean, listening to the waves, and taking a moment to exhale life.

Those moments are priceless.

So, for my speech therapist to be so caring and understanding about my suffering meant a lot, and our outside sessions rejuvenated my soul and encouraged me to keep pushing. She and I would work on things like memory, pronunciation, and writing skills. She was a young lady with a pure heart and selflessly dedicated to seeing me do well.

We did a variety of exercises together. She would say a phrase and have me say the phrase back to her. I would try to repeat the phrase while forcing myself to talk slowly and be understood. I also had to do activities that required me to describe everyday objects on a sheet of paper and try to spell and sound them out. I remember trying so hard to get those things right the first time. Some of the objects looked familiar, but to articulate my answer was an entirely different story. I had trouble repeating the phrases back to her and found that I needed her to repeat them for me to retain the information.

As a few days went by, my speech started to improve. I was able to recite words to my therapist and speak a bit more clearly. Then, one day, she had instructed me to take a moment and write my name. I was also instructed to write the medications I would be taking, how many pills each day, and what days I was to take each prescription. I began this task, but as soon as I started, my heart fell deeper into my chest. You see, my penmanship wasn't the greatest before unless I took my time to write, and now, my writing was horrible. I looked at my blank piece of paper, and all I could do was cry. There I was, a grown man, and I couldn't write my name.

I wiped my tears, straightened up a bit, and grasped the pen to give it a shot. As I began writing, I realized, yet again, that my writing looked like a child learning penmanship for the first time, and I had to quickly accept that I needed to relearn this task, too. My mind jogged back to the times I took for granted – quickly writing down a grocery list, doodling on a spare piece of scratch paper, and signing the bill at a restaurant.

I didn't want to give up or not try, but, admittedly, I wanted results, and I wanted them now. My therapist wouldn't let me remain discouraged, though. Of course, she gave me the space to have my moments of discouragement, but she never let me stay in that place. Day in and day out, we met for a therapy session, and we really started seeing results. Little by little, my writing and motor skills were improving.

"Baby steps," I had told myself, and ironically, I was at the stage in my life when I was experiencing a rebirth – learning skills for the first time, aiming higher, and reaching for my goal with the same ferocity a young child exhibits when trying to take their first steps or tie their shoes. Our meetings lasted for about an hour, and although that seems short, they were intense.

Thanksgiving rolled around, and I was still in the hospital but without mandated therapy, because the staff was off for the holiday. As I sat in my bed, watching the famous Macy's Thanksgiving Day Parade on television, sadness crept in my spirit. With no one in sight, I began speaking aloud. "This isn't how it was supposed to be," I quietly cried. "This is the year I was finally able to go and see the parade in person," I reminded myself aloud.

Before my stroke, I was so excited about the coming year because I knew I would be in New York during Thanksgiving, so I could attend the parade in person, something that has been on my bucket list for quite some time. These feelings were hard to digest, not only because I felt sad about my current state but also because I felt guilty for feeling sad in the first place. I was incredibly thankful to be alive, no longer in ICU, and making great strides, but I was heartbroken that my life was at a standstill. I wanted God to know I appreciate Him, yet I also prayed (and pleaded) that He would expedite this phase in my life and transition me into the life I knew before – a life with physical freedoms.

I had many conversations with God throughout those days in the hospital, both silently and aloud. On Thanksgiving Day, as I was talking to Him, something happened out of nowhere, something I had been waiting to happen. It was like when Moses saw the burning bush, and this sign brought Moses assurance that He was near and always by his side. I experienced a profound moment of divine intervention because, as I was praying, my voice came back. During this time of prayer, which at one point was inaudible, I was able to speak in a normal tone. My words slurred a bit, but had someone been in the room, they would've understood me clearly. I was able to make coherent sounds again! Never in a million years did I think hearing my voice would be such a monumental moment in my life, but this was one of the most wondrous times to date.

God knew my heart.

He knew I was hurting, yet He knew I

was grateful.

He knows we are flawed, and He knows we struggle with control – wanting our way opposed to accepting His timing – and I thank Him for leading me to experience this indescribable joy.

After the holiday, I resumed therapy sessions. I could've burst in anticipation, as I could hardly wait to reveal my big surprise to my therapist, the person who had stuck by my side since my first day of therapy. Unbeknown to her, my voice was back, and she was in for a major surprise.

That day, she greeted me with her usual bright smile. "Good morning, Anthony!" she had said, to which I smiled but didn't speak yet.

As she inched closer to me to take her seat, tears of joy formed in the corners of my eyes, and I knew it was time to reveal my secret.

"Good morning," I clearly said with a

huge smile plastered across my face.

She was stunned. She couldn't believe it! Her face was painted with the same joy that filled my spirit. With her eyes as big as quarters and a smile that showed every pearly white tooth in her mouth, she began asking me a million questions. "When did this happen? How are you feeling? Can you speak a bit more?"

Then, with much excitement, she notified the doctors, nurses, and team of therapists of the good news. I was speaking again, and this was the spark I needed to keep my fire lit as I worked toward a full recovery.

CHAPTER SIX

"Being confident of this that he who began a good work in you will carry it on to completion until the day of Christ Jesus."

Philippians 1:6

The day I spoke to my speech therapist, it felt as if the heavens were singing from above, and although this was a special moment, I knew the marathon needed to continue. Working towards regaining my short-term memory and refreshing certain life skills were my new goals with my occupational therapist. Thanks be to God, my long-term memory was intact, yet my short-term memory was completely off-kilter. My therapist would tell me something, and in a matter of minutes, I would forget, as if those words were never spoken. This was difficult because in order to progress, I needed to retain information. With the doctors informing me of my next steps, medications, and progress updates, I needed to be able to keep that information and use it to take the necessary steps towards prevention, maintenance, and wellness. Because my short-term memory wasn't cooperating, I needed to write everything, and this presented a problem because my writing skills had yet to come back in the way my voice had returned. Thanks to technology, I used my smartphone and created a section for notes. Typing came easier than writing, so this was a great temporary solution to my memory issue. At the time, I was so focused on regaining these basic skills that I forgot about the idea of recording information. Nevertheless, my therapist and I started working toward regaining my coordination skills.

One strengthening exercise involved a board of lights. In the rehab treatment room, I would approach the board of lights on the back wall. These lights would light up with colors of yellow, green, and red, and my therapist would go to the computer to create sounds and patterns out of the lights. It was up to me to remember the pattern and recreate it. The lights also created random patterns, and I would have to catch the light before it went away. Despite the difficulty of the light board, I was up for the challenge. The board was about the size of a 70-inch flat-screen TV, and the lights covered the board. Upon my therapist's directions, I began to chase the lights at the top of the screen, but the next set of lights was at the bottom. I wasn't reaching all the lights, but I was able to make valiant attempts. At this time, I was unable to stand, so I would sit in the wheelchair and maneuver at my best. I stopped to take breaks because holding my arm for long periods was exhausting. As I would go to the next level, the patterns started to become more complex with longer pattern sequences, and some sequences sped up as well. I was tired and drained, but I knew this exercise was helping my focus, endurance, and reflexes.

As I regained strength and coordination, my exercises intensified and changed. Yet again, my therapist tapped into my love for the outdoors and created a therapy session outside. Now using a walker, I was presented with new therapy exercises. Using a walker was a major milestone, and moving away from needing a wheelchair felt liberating, yet I continued to suffer from pain in my leg while I used my walker. Throughout every step of my therapy journey, I circled back to God and my faith. Ironically, as my challenges in therapy intensified, so did my faith. I knew God had everything worked out. I just needed to endure these challenges to get my life back.

My therapist had escorted me to the hospital herb garden, and I was thrilled to be outside, especially surrounded by such lovely scents. In fact, the scents were nostalgic. In high school, I utilized our career center, which allowed students to explore trades, and I pursued the culinary arts route for two years. During my last semester, the instructor introduced us to baking and pastry arts, where we learned to make basic home desserts, pies, and cakes. Every Friday, we learned to make chocolates and participated in cake decorating. I fell in love with this art form and wanted to pursue a career in pastries. This passion led to a diploma and certification in Culinary Arts and a degree from Johnson & Wales University. Nevertheless, that day, my therapist and I walked to the herb garden, and she wanted me to identify the herbs. Each label was covered, so I was to break a small piece of the herb, smell it, and tell her its name. The garden was filled with an array of herbs – rosemary, dill, cilantro, basil, oregano, thyme, parsley, mint, and bay leaves. As I gently bent over to smell each plant, my memory was sparked with vivid images, and I was easily able to identify mint, bay leaves, oregano, rosemary, and basil. My mind reverted to the incredible memories of being in the kitchen, creating meals at work and cooking for my loved ones.

My beef stir fry over rice was always my

friends' favorite.

My lasagna filled guests up with nothin' but love.

My white chocolate strawberry cheesecake had people begging for more.

I've created winning desserts that earned two scholarships from Johnson & Wales University – low-fat orange cranberry mini bread load and a mandarin orange cheesecake.

Food occupies a giant space in my heart and mind, and being in this garden jogged my memory further than I imagined. Although the smells were familiar, some of the names weren't recognizable. Instead of panicking or succumbing to my frustration, I closed my eyes and relied on other senses to figure this out. At the end of this exercise, I was able to identify every herb, without the assistance of my therapist.

Anthony – 1
Stroke – 0.

CHAPTER SEVEN

"You may encounter many defeats, but you must not be defeated. In fact, it may be necessary to encounter the defeats, so you can know who you are, what you can rise from, how you can still come out of it."

Maya Angelou

Within five days of working tirelessly at the rehab facility, I was able to move around the room and hospital without a wheelchair. Thank God because being in a wheelchair was exhausting. Having to use your upper body to maneuver requires a lot of focus and strength. I found myself short-winded, trying to move from Point A to Point B, but never gave up. My heart already went out to individuals in wheelchairs, but after having to be in one, my admiration level grew dramatically. Temporary wheelchair confinement was a total life adjustment, and I never saw myself having to be in that physical space.

The staff saw my work and determination, which they fully supported. Their actions and excitement to see me win and beat this, along with the love and support of my friends and family, fueled me to another level. I went to each therapy session and gave my all, despite doctors telling me that I may still need bypass surgery. They even mentioned that I might need a peacemaker or stints in my heart to help keep it on track. I processed this new information as an opportunity to trust God and believe Him to get me out of this. There was no way I was going to be 39 years old, living the rest of my life dependent upon a machine to make my heart work. Absolutely not! I know who my Father is, and there was no way He would leave me like that. My faith has never waivered from knowing the truth of His power. I know that the stories we read in the Bible are true and that they can and are happening now, too, but in the form of other people. The same God who created me was going to be the same God who healed me and restored my health. I've seen miracles performed in the lives of many, and I knew a miracle would happen in my life, too. God created my heart to function in a perfect state. Therefore, I believed that He was going to revive me to a fully functioning state again. I've never been one to doubt His ability, never believing anything other than whatever He created, He can do again. If He cares enough to allow a salamander to lose a limb but regenerate a new one, surely He cares for me to make my heart work without a machine. In Luke 12:22-31, Jesus said to His disciples:

> Therefore I tell you, do not worry about your life, what you will eat, or about your body, what you will wear. For life is more than food, and the body more than clothes. Consider the ravens: They do not sow or reap, they have no storeroom or barn; yet GOD feeds them. And how much more valuable you are than birds! Who of you by worrying can add a single hour to your life? Since you cannot do this very little thing, why do you worry about the rest? Consider how the wildflowers grow. They do not labor or spin. Yet I tell you, not even Solomon in all his splendor

was dressed like one of these. If that is how God clothes the grass in the field, which is here today, and tomorrow is thrown into the fire, how much more will HE clothe you-you of little faith! And do not set your heart on what you will eat or drink; do not worry about it. For the pagan world runs after all such things and your Father knows that you need them. But seek His kingdom, and these things will be given to you as well.

As I recited those verses during my stay in rehab, I realized this was my chance to really put my faith to work and believe His Word.

I continued to work with my therapist to get my life back. At every session, I gave my all and focused on results. I went from being in a wheelchair to using a walker. Then, after a few short days after learning how to use the walker, I was given a cane. They wanted to see how I would get around with minimal support. I tried to walk with the cane but found it very challenging. While walking with a cane, you must move the cane at the same time as the opposite leg. This was a difficult task because I couldn't get my brain to register the movements. Each time I walked, I walked with the cane on my right side and would move it with my right leg. Finally, after a day of trying, I threw the cane to the side and requested that the therapist teach me to walk without it. This was a big move, seeing that my balance still wasn't that great, but I was up for the challenge. Therapists would strap a support belt around my chest to hold me. We went through the hallway, and I started my attempt to walk, but couldn't move quickly due to being nervous without support. Initially, I walked close to the wall. Even though the therapist held me, I wanted extra reinforcement. Before my stroke, both places that I resided in, New York and Charleston, had stairs, so we worked on trying to go up and down the stairs.

The first steps were a set of six. I would have to go up, down the other side, and then back the way I came. I felt very accomplished and had little fear. The next session presented a bigger challenge. I was taken to the stairwell and asked to make it up and down the stairs. There had to have been about 20 to 25 steps. During my first attempt, I was allowed to go up and down while holding the rail. The next time, I had to go up without any help from the therapist. I got to the bottom of the stairs, took a deep breath, and assured myself I could do this. I took my first step and was a bit shaken but had to get past that feeling. I moved on to the next step, and before I knew it, I was at the top of the stairs. I couldn't stop smiling as both therapists stood below, clapping and cheering for me. After realizing I could do it, I went down the stairs with no problem. I got to the bottom and gave both therapists a huge hug. That day, I walked back from that session with no help at all. During the next session, I walked through the hospital with the therapist by my side to ensure that I wouldn't fall. As I was walking around, two of my loved ones came to see me. They just so happened to come in while I was walking freely on my own. The look on their faces brought joy to my heart. They were super excited to see this miracle taking place.

As the days went by, I focused on my coordination skills. I was to try and catch a tennis ball as my therapist bounced it to me. Sometimes, we would stand further apart as they bounced it to me, and I needed to focus. I had to play with shapes and try to put the shapes in the corresponding parts of the board. To regain strength in my hand, I would take clay, stretch it out with one hand, and form it back into a ball. This was going to help me with regaining my grip. I also worked with colored clothespins, having to take each color and clip it to the corresponding color on the puzzle board. I hated this activity. Tedious tasks or anything redundant made it hard to concentrate. I would have to search for a specific color paper clip in a glass jar that was filled with other regular colored paperclips. Once I found the colors, I had to connect the colored paper clips. I found this to be very annoying, but did it, especially because I knew my results and progress were monitored closely.

CHAPTER EIGHT

"My scars remind me that I did, indeed, survive my deepest wounds. That, in itself, is an accomplishment. And they bring to mind something else, too. They remind me that the damage life has inflicted on me has, in many places, left me stronger and more resilient. What hurt me in the past has actually made me better equipped to face the present."

Steve Goodier

It was the week after Thanksgiving of 2018, and I was still at this rehabilitation center.

However, my voice had started coming back even stronger, I was able to walk on my own, and my short-term memory seemed to be improving. Once I got to the rehab facility, my time with God became more purposeful. There was always a conversation going on within me, mainly geared toward having my health restored and without lasting effects. Since the ocean, one of my happy places, wasn't within reach, I would lay in bed, every day, and listen to some of my favorite songs and think about how great it would be to function normally again. I played one song every day to remind me of His strength, and I sang this song to remind Him I knew of His strength. Every day, I would play Pastor William Murphy's "You Are My Strength." Although my voice was back, I was unable to sing, couldn't hold a tune at all, but it was just God and me in the room, so there was no one to judge me. As awful as I sounded, I would belt out the words:

> *"You are my strength, strength like no other.*
> *Strength like no other reaches to me.*
> *In the fullness of Your grace, in the power of*
> *Your name, You lift me up, You lift me up."*

The lyrics ran through my spirit as I sang unto the Lord. With every word, I felt my faith intensify, and I knew He could not only hear me but feel my heart, too.

One day, as I was having my time with God, one of the hospital workers, an older southern woman, walked into my room. I wasn't paying attention to the time of day, but she was there to bring my dinner. I didn't even notice that she came in and caught my attempt to sing.

"Baby," she said. "You keep on worshipping God! He is the One that's going to heal you and see you through this. I'll sit your food right over here. You just continue to worship, and you can eat when you're ready."

With tears in my eyes, I looked at her and said, "Yes, ma'am, and thank you!"

Her spirit reminded me so much of my grandmother, and to feel her energy during that pivotal time in my life was incredible. In the Black American community, especially in the south, grandmothers are the cornerstone of families. They take on many roles and give unparalleled love and support. My grandmother was one of my best friends, and her love still lives with me today. She passed away a few weeks after I graduated high school, which was something she desired to see me accomplish. The hospital staffer who delivered my food knew God and my situation, and what she said to me felt as though God sent her to remind me that He hears me. After our brief encounter, I felt affirmed, I knew I would be alright, I would make it, and I would be whole again.

I started working on at-home functions and looking toward life after rehab, being sure to shower on my own and handle grooming tasks. The staff wanted to ensure I could handle a range of everyday tasks at home – bathing, brushing my teeth, cooking, feeding myself, and so forth. A therapist was also assigned to test my driving skills. I went into a room where a computer was set up that featured a simulated car. It had a steering wheel and foot pedals, just like one of those race cars at the arcade. I sat in front of the computer, and on the screen was a setup just like a racing game where there was a car on the road and a few pedestrians. As she gave instructions on how to operate the program, I became excited but nervous. My nerves came into play because my coordination had increased a great deal, but I hadn't been behind the wheel in months.

Getting behind the wheel, although it was only a game, presented a challenge. So, I listened to her instructions and pressed start. On the screen, the controls told me the goal at hand, and I would try to reach it. I would have to pass other vehicles properly, stop for the people crossing the street, park in various spaces, and focus on staying in the lane. With each attempt, I was getting better and better. By the time we finished, I had gotten the hang of it, but my reaction time to other cars and pedestrians was not so great. When we finished, my therapist let me know that I needed to increase my reaction time for when I needed to brake, and that was the only feedback I received in terms of room for improvement. Although that was the only feedback, that was something I needed to strengthen because God forbid I hurt anyone while driving.

CHAPTER NINE

"Making each day count like it's your last day to
fulfill your dreams, is unarguably the master key to a
future full of great rewards."
Edmond Mbiaka

With so much progress happening, getting the okay to go home was on the horizon. I went from not being able to do anything on my own to being self-sufficient in many areas. Moving around freely was a huge feat. I fought tooth and nail to win back my physical independence. To ensure the strength of my heart and ability to function outside of rehab, the doctors wanted to run a few more tests. I received a few more X-rays of my heart and another stress test to measure the functioning rate of my heart. The doctors discovered that my heart was pumping the blood it needed to function, but I only had about 20% use of it. They told me that once I was able to go home, I needed more physical therapy and speech therapy.

I was to go to therapy three times a week and have a one-hour session with each therapist. I was to stay on my current medications and go to the doctor twice a week to ensure that my blood levels were normal and that my iron was in a good place. Being on Warfarin causes your blood to be all over the place. My international normalized ratio level (INR) needed to stay between one and two. If not, my doses would need to be adjusted. I would also have to start exercising again. I exercised before this ordeal and saw great results, but at this stage of my life, I wasn't interested in doing that. Having a stroke drastically changed my life, and my world revolved around therapy, restrictions, and relearning basic movements, so to add a strict exercise schedule was daunting. I wanted to eat what I wanted and not be confined to a certain diet. Although what I wanted was against doctors' orders, I had no intention of falling in that unhealthy trap. This was a matter of life and death, and I chose life. My doctors had provided me with papers that had pictures and written instructions on what type of exercises I should perform. I wasn't going to be able to lift any weights, only do cardio. They feared that the stress from the weightlifting would put too much pressure on my heart.

I've battled with my weight for some years now. Growing up, I wasn't very athletic. I dabbled in sports, participating in the community basketball team and church baseball team. In middle school, I tried out for the basketball team and didn't make the cut, so I became their cameraman. Then, I finally worked up the courage to try out for the football team.

Well, that was short-lived.

When we had to go on to the field, geared up with pads and a helmet, I found myself extremely uncomfortable. It was hot, and I felt like I couldn't breathe. I went to the doctor and had a physical, and the results showed a heart murmur. So, I was not allowed to participate in football.

Listen – that news didn't disappoint me by any means. In fact, I was happy. I'm claustrophobic and don't care for hot weather, so being in the heat and having to wear a helmet made me feel as though I was closed in – not a winning combination. Instead, I signed up for other activities like student council and various groups at school, which kept me occupied.

Also, while growing up, my weight was average, but society certainly plays a part in how you are viewed and should view yourself. I wasn't sculpted and didn't have a six-pack. When seeing the jocks at school, I was quite envious of their physique. During those middle school years, life seemed to throw many battles my way. I learned that the man I had been calling "dad" wasn't my father, and I resented my mother for denying that part of me. I also felt inadequate because I didn't look the way society deemed attractive. I felt like a letdown because I wasn't the athlete my family wanted me to be, and I was navigating in a new, uncomfortable financial space. My mother had sustained an injury at work that left her unable to perform her duties. Then, her job ending up laying off the staff. We weren't wealthy, but we weren't poor. I was accustomed to doing activities at school, like field trips and obtaining choral attire with no problems of having my family take care of it, especially my mom. Being the only male in the house, I wanted to help in some way so we could maintain a normal life. I wore a happy mask on the outside, yet I became depressed. For six months, I dealt with depression, suicidal thoughts, and bulimia. This was my secret war, and I had to fight through it to survive.

In the black community, issues like these are looked down upon and not discussed. Then, add being a male to that equation, and we are taught never to show emotion or have these feelings. This is an unfortunate mentality

104

to have and allow to continue. The reality is people go through turmoil and need help getting past certain issues and feelings. Yes, loving God, going to church, and knowing His Word are great, but people need more than a Sunday message to work through their issues. People often say that kids shouldn't carry those burdens, but I was affected by a multitude of stressors.

Today, we see more youth turning to other outlets of pain because they have no one to talk to about their problems and feelings. These issues are real, not fleeting, and need to be addressed, whether male or female, white, black, brown, or yellow, rich or poor, religious or not, straight, gay, bisexual, or transgender. No matter who or what you are, you deserve to be heard. I suffered in silence, which led to exhibiting an attitude toward others. Not being able to share my voice, in fear that the world would say that a black male should never show any emotions, was debilitating.

In therapy, when I was told I needed to exercise, I began to examine my past feelings about my weight, and they came rushing back. I had to set aside these thoughts, prepare my mind for my new journey, and commit to making fitness a part of my life. I was to exercise at least three to four times a week, whether I used the elliptical or treadmill, outdoor bicycle, or whatever I needed to get my body moving for at least 15 minutes a day. The more weight I was to lose, the better my chances were to have a healthier life.

Soon thereafter, after all the tests came back clear, I received the news that I was able to go home and continue with outpatient rehab. A dietician came to my room to talk to me about my meals outside of the hospital. She took me through how to reach the best results by eating a lot of the good stuff – fruits, raw vegetables, and lean meats – and drinking lots of water. She gave me different meal options to try to keep it fresh.

The following Monday, I was to go to one final round of meetings with my therapist as well as talk to the doctors about my medicine schedule and follow-up appointments. I was set to be out of there that afternoon. My ride, more like my escape car, had been set and was going to take me home. I appreciated my brother being there for me and getting me out of there. The sessions that day couldn't happen fast enough. I had been in this hospital for almost a month, and the thought of having to stay in this facility any longer made me sick to my core. I needed to get out of there and be free. I needed to lay in my own bed, use my own bathroom, and freely step outside to enjoy the fresh air. I needed to be free.

As my brother and I headed back to my place, I felt excited about walking up the stairs and being in my bedroom. This felt great, although I was also struck with memories of my first stroke. At that moment, my life had changed so fast, and here it was changing again.

My funds were low because I had been out of work, and I needed to get started with the right items for my new journey, which included purchasing healthy food. Many people came together to help me buy the food I needed and to get my medications, which were very costly due to no insurance. Thankfully, my insurance was going to be active in one month.

Four days after being released from rehab, I was getting ready to start my first outpatient session. It felt good to know that I wasn't too far away from making a complete recovery. I went to my first session, which was physical therapy. My therapist wanted me to start with exercises that involved using my legs. At this time, the concern wasn't my leg being weak. My concern was that the pain in my right leg had moved to my left leg. Before we did anything, my therapist had me lay on a table. She then massaged my legs and feet. As a former massage therapist, knowing the power of touch, I was in therapeutic heaven. We applied some ice packs on my legs, and the pain seemed to subside. We began the session by taking a huge bouncing ball and walking back and forth while dribbling the ball. I lost the ball a couple of times but was able to run to retrieve it and get back on track. Then, I did some cardio on the stationary bicycle. Each session involved some type of cardio in getting my blood flowing, followed by various activities such as bouncing a tennis ball against the wall that had a target in the middle. For that exercise, my job was to hit the target and catch the ball as it bounced back. I would have to walk across a balance beam while encountering different heights of stairs. All these exercises helped increase my ability to respond with my reflexes. I found the challenges not too terribly difficult. At this point, all my energy was put into living a normal life.

In my speech therapy session, she worked with me on how to properly speak by making sure I was over-pronouncing words and speaking at a pace that would allow me to be understood. I would also have to recite a list of five random words. I would close my eyes as she would call out the words, and I'd try my best to make the words relate somehow. I had to say them back to her in the exact order she had said. In the beginning, this was quite difficult because these five words had nothing to do with each other, so I was unable to make the words coordinate. Over time, I found a way to say them in my head and then recite them aloud. There were one or two words I would have trouble saying, but ultimately said them all.

I also had to work on computing basic math without a calculator or paper. This was to test my thinking skills and to help with my processing abilities. The great thing about this exercise is that I was able to do the calculations immediately. I've never been a math whiz but having worked with money for several years, I'm able to tell you the change due, so I thought of the numbers as cash, and everything went okay from there.

Both of those sessions went on for weeks, and I worked on these exercises repeatedly. Then, on Friday, December 21, 2018, I went to my physical therapy session as usual. We started with some cardio for about

15 minutes before proceeding with the activities for the day. I had started to do the tasks she asked, and at that moment, she looked at me and requested I stop. With a puzzled look on my face, I stopped and sat.

"I would like you to hold on, please," she said as she turned to her computer and began typing.

With each keystroke, I wondered what she was about to do or say. It was near the end of the month, and I wanted to get back to work, which meant I wanted to go hard at these therapy sessions. I had hoped she wasn't going to tell me that I need to continue with more weeks of rehab. I just didn't want to hear that at all. I also thought that she might tell me I'm pushing myself too hard and need to slow down. I didn't know what to think, but my mind wandered into different territories. Sitting there, waiting for her to say something, was agonizing.

Ten minutes later, she proceeded to turn her attention to me, and as she looked at me with a stern face, she spoke. "I was just emailing your doctor," she said.

I continued to listen, bracing myself for awful news.

"I was letting your doctor know that you no longer need to be here. The exercises I gave you today were actually for an evaluation test, and you passed with flying colors, so there was no need for you to continue the test! I let your doctor know that you can be released from therapy and that you're able to return to work."

I couldn't believe the news.

I was stunned, elated, and at a loss of words.

Then, she looked at me with joy in her eyes and said, "Just know you're one of the lucky ones."

The fear I felt moments ago turned to celebratory claps and cheers. My prayers had been answered, and I was free to go back to my life with a new sense of ambition, determination, and drive.

"Thank you!" I said. "I'm very aware of how blessed I am, and I won't take this for granted."

With tears in our eyes, we hugged, and then I ran out of there. I couldn't run far though, because I still had to go to speech therapy. On my way to speech therapy, I wondered if I would have to stay in South Carolina for speech sessions. I silently questioned how much longer I would have to go to speech and if I could do it in New York. That way, I could return to work and continue treatment.

Although I received miraculous news at physical therapy, I went into speech therapy with mixed emotions. I had greeted my therapist, and she immediately congratulated me on my recent news that she heard from the other staff member. She told me that today's session was simply to go over some things to ensure I'm ready for life after my stroke. We discussed how I needed to maintain keeping my words clear, over pronouncing and not speaking fast. We went over some exercises to strengthen my voice, like warming up for a musical performance. This was to help with the overall delivery of my speech.

"Your overall progress has been great," she said, "and there are a few things that will work themselves out over time, but your time with me has come to an end."

More music to my ears!

This was a monumental day in my life. With a smile on her face, she looked at me and happily said, "Congratulations! You're released from therapy."

That day, my prayers and affirmations came true. I was free to be me again, and this is a feeling I won't forget as long as I live.

CHAPTER TEN

"And we know that all things work together for the good to them that love God, to them who are the called according to his purpose."

Romans 8:28

There I was, the Monday after getting the news of my release to return to work, waiting for my doctors to send my final paperwork so I could send these documents to my job. My mind was racing as I tried to wait patiently for things to be handled. Although my nerves were elevated, I was still on Cloud 9 as I prepared to transition to my previous life. I knew I had so many things to do to make this transition work.

I needed to find a gym that I could use regularly. I also needed to schedule appointments with my general physician and cardiologists. My doctors said I wouldn't need a cardiologist in New York, but I needed a physician so they could communicate with each other on my progress. I also needed to find a place in New York so that I could continue having blood work at least once a week to monitor my blood levels and overall progress. Luckily, the pharmacy I was using is nationwide, so access to my medications would be a breeze. That was one less thing I needed to handle.

Later that afternoon, I finally received my paperwork and sent it off to my job for clearance. My employer was very supportive during my time of leave and had even asked me if I wanted to wait and take more time off. Although that was a very kind gesture, I was determined to be up and running. Staying out any longer wasn't an option.

Two days later, my employer had notified me that everything was processed and ready to go, and I would be back on the schedule starting January 1st. I have always been dedicated to my work, so receiving a return date felt incredible. Going back to work was most important to me, not only because I love my job, but because it proved I beat the odds. This set date was the manifestation of my beliefs fully functioning again. I thought about times in the past when I worked many jobs at once. At one point, I worked two jobs while attending high school. Through the Culinary Arts Program, I was able to work at a local grocery as a cake decorator. I had finished most of my credits, so I only had two classes in the morning, and after class, I went to work. I would work until about six in the evening, and then I would work at a local restaurant at night. I did this about four to five times a week. I was able to work and remain involved with the honors chorus, student council, and other extra-curricular activities such as church groups and choir, still managing to come out of school with my diploma.

I made plans to leave Charleston, South Carolina, before New Year's Eve, so I could make sure I was settled in and ready for work. Normally, I wouldn't work or have anything to do with work on New Year's Eve or New Year's Day. However, this time was different. My life had been interrupted long enough, so having to not participate in any of the NYE festivities or working on the day after didn't bother me at all because I was happy to bring in the New Year at work.

When I arrived back at the Concrete Jungle, I was met with so much love from my roommates and coworkers. It felt good to be back and even better to have such love poured into me from everyone. I thought to myself, "Wow, Anthony! You're really here, and what came to destroy you didn't win. You stood firm and crushed it." I had to take a moment for myself and celebrate being back after all I endured.

You can go days without realizing how simple things matter most in life. We are abundantly blessed and must keep that in perspective. Everyday challenges come, and we often become consumed with the weight of it all that we lose sight of our fortunes and blessings. Amid everything I endured, I still remembered there was someone somewhere going through worse than me. The fact that I had air in my lungs and was able to be in my right mind were reasons to give thanks. Each day, we must make a conscious effort to remember the good things in life. Everything that transpires, good and bad, are small parts of our story, but how we forge on and live is the glory of the story.

There are so many ways my story could've gone:

I could not have regained my short-term memory.

I could not have walked again.

I could have needed open-heart surgery, bypass surgery, or a pacemaker.

Worse, I could have died, unable to share my story.

But God saw fit for my life to go another way! I thank God for providing His healing power to save my life. He is and will always be an ever-present help in my life. God worked so many miracles that I still feel in awe, to this day, of His favor over my life.

***

The medical bills started to come in quickly, and boy, there was so much money owed. I believed it would take a lifetime to pay off those bills. Despite the overwhelming debt, I refused to be irresponsible and not pay anything towards the bills I accumulated. Admittedly, that mindset was not the attitude I used to have towards taking care of bills and not going into debt. A lot had changed to cause me to get out of that old mindset.

Throughout the years, several factors made me not worry about going into debt. I was never taught how to obtain wealth and good credit, which are vital lessons in life that everyone should know. All I knew was that if you have money, you should spend it. There's a saying that goes, "robbing Peter to pay Paul." Basically, this expression means taking money from one place and applying it to another, although you need to pay that very thing you just took from. I now believe and understand I need to be Peter because he had enough for Paul to rob him. So, I shall have, and unlike Peter, I will not lose it or be robbed of it. I declare that one day I will be debt-free and wealthy. I pray I will continue to have a mindset of a good steward over what is given to me. In Luke 16:10, the Bible states, "He that is faithful in that which is least is faithful also in much: and he that is unjust in the least is unjust also in much." So, I'm putting forth the effort to fix what I created with what little I have been given and remain faithful that it will become more in the future. Although I had those medical bills, I wasn't stressed about the amount. I should've been, but I knew that He took care of me through this whole ordeal and that He would continue to provide.

While I was out of work, not only did I not have any medical insurance, but I was without short-term and long-term disability, too. I only had a few days of PTO, which I was able to use, but I had nothing else. By law, in the state of New York, they must provide workers with some type of coverage while they're out of work for medical leave. I had to live off $125 a week, the total amount provided, and that ended the last week of December. This was hard because all my bills were still coming in and due. Some collectors were willing to work with my circumstances and hold off on billing me, but others, not so much. Although I had the money for November bills, because I was prepared for that month, paying December, January, and February were going to be a stretch to handle. However, the way my village came together and helped me was overwhelming. I lacked nothing and did not have to ask for anything, not a dime! This level of generosity, love, support, and consideration is indescribable. To think that the people in my life loved me so much that they prioritized my bills and financial well-being is more than I could ever imagine.

My total hospital stay came out to $130,000, and that was after the charitable contributions for my rehabilitation treatments. I called the financial department of the hospital and let them know I was just returning to work and wouldn't be able to put a lot toward this debt, but I wanted to pay them something towards the account. It may seem silly, but I offered to pay $10 a month for the first few months and planned to increase the amount in the future. To my surprise, they agreed to it and even said I could start in February. So, I called them in February to make my first payment. When the lady pulled up my account, she read the balance owed and asked how much I would like to pay, but the balance she read was way off from what I knew I owed.

The balance was $1,000.

Feeling a bit concerned, I asked her to please review the account because owing $1,000 didn't make sense.

"Sir, that's the correct amount. Apparently, the hospital took care of the rest," she explained.

I was in sheer disbelief.

Over $129,000 had been covered on my behalf, and I couldn't process this news. I was elated!

I made the monthly payment

arrangement and vowed to continue paying until my debt was gone. My Father in Heaven provided me with such favor, and there was nothing more I could even begin to ask for in this life. In March, however, a whole other blessing was waiting for me when I called the hospital to pay my bill.

The woman from the finance office had pulled up my account information and informed me that I had a balance of $100. Stunned by this news, I asked her to please make sure she was looking at the right account. I let her know that last month, I was told I was responsible for $1,000 and had only paid $10 towards that.

"Yes, sir, I see your payment from last month, but your account balance is only $100. How would you like to pay?" she continued.

"You can take all of it right now!" I quickly replied.

She processed the payment, and I then asked her to send the paid-in-full records via email. I was shocked yet thrilled by what just took place, but I wasn't going to be anybody's fool and not have receipts to vouch for it, just in case they claimed a computer glitch.

Blessings on blessings on blessings!

God made sure that the burden of this ordeal would not weigh me down.

Do I get things right in life?

Certainly not all the time.

Have I fallen short of His grace?

Yes, more times than I can count.

Yet His undying love for me has kept me alive. My purpose and destiny have yet to be fulfilled, and in knowing that, I want to glorify His name and swiftly move toward my calling. The love I have for Him is real, and He knows that.

Since birth, death and disaster have tried

to take me off this Earth. I remember my mom telling me about what the doctors told her to do when she arrived home with me. For whatever reason, and until this day, I have no idea why, but the hospital staff instructed her to toss me on my head on the bed three times. This does not make any sense whatsoever, yet medical professionals instructed my mom to do this. Tossing me on my head could have caused major head trauma, a broken neck, or paralyzation, yet here I am, alive and well, and I'm grateful for that.

Since I've been home and living life, I've been able to stop taking Warfarin. This has allowed me to eat green leafy vegetables again. My salads are even better with this addition. Also, my speaking voice has fully returned, and at times, I find myself talking faster than I should and needing to slow my words so people can understand me. Who would've thought?! Although speech therapy helped me get my voice back, it didn't help me regain my ability to sing. My vocals were shot. Only two of my friends knew that I went to see a vocal coach for lessons. Those three months proved to work as I am now able to carry a tune or two. This feels wonderful because music is and will always be a huge part of my life. I'm still on a health journey, and though I have some pounds to go, I can say I have achieved a great deal along the way. I continue to do cardio about three or four times a week, and I continue to eat healthy options, although I did start to treat myself now and then. I had bought some peanut butter cups, one of my favorite candy. I normally would buy two king-sized packs, but I decided only to buy a regular pack to avoid falling back into old habits. I know all things need to be done in moderation, so I forced myself only to buy one. To know that I finally could control my sweet tooth was a huge feat.

I like to joke and say that I have lost a whole human. I went down five shirt and pants sizes and lost over 90 pounds. Eating right and working out have become a way of life. I have vowed to live every day to the fullest. I've also learned to appreciate one of my social media networks for their memories that pop up on my wall – memories of old statuses and photos. They remind me of all I've done and seen, and I realize I now live with purpose, and a basic life is no longer the answer. Having a new outlook on life has challenged me to try and conqueror feats I normally would be fearful to attempt.

On a trip to Barbados in February of 2020, I finally dared to go snorkeling in the crystal-clear water. I've always loved the water but would never take my feet off the bottom of the ocean floor. It wasn't until 2010 that I learned how to swim. I was paralyzed by fear, just thinking that that water could envelop me. I can follow and submit to a swim instructor, but I still felt like I had no control of the water. Despite failed lessons, I knew that I loved the water and needed to learn once and for all. Finally, through one of my clients, I found a highly recommended instructor, and she was wonderful. We had private sessions where she would take great care in meeting my needs. Within four weeks, I finally learned to swim. I would jump in a pool, go underwater, and swim my little heart out.

Four years after those lessons, on a cruise with my cousins, one of our stops was in the Grand Cayman Islands. I couldn't resist the beauty of the ocean. The water was so clear that you could see for miles. Me, one of my cousins, and one of her friends decided to go snorkeling, but when I reached the edge, I chickened out. There wasn't any walking out on the sand to get adjusted to the water, either. We were to go to the edge by the rocks and then climb down a ladder to get into the water. The water was a bit above my waist, but I didn't like being unable to walk in and get my body acclimated to the water.

Well, I went down the ladder to give it another try and still couldn't bring myself to get in the water. At this point, I was able to see the beautiful schools of fish and harmless nurse sharks, an amazing sight to see. I was still feeling afraid, so I gave my cousin and her friend the go-ahead to get in the water without me. They went out for a little while and came back to check on me. They then suggested I go out with them to see the awesome water. Still having doubts, I said, "no," but that quickly changed. I heard this little voice yelling,

"Daddy! Daddy, look at me." I looked over, and a little girl was snorkeling in the water with others. I immediately felt so upset with myself that I wouldn't get myself together to get in the water. I finally looked at my cousins and jokingly said, "There's no way I'm going to let this little girl show me up!" So, I gave my cousin the "yes" for us to go.

"If I tap you twice, please bring me back to shore," I told her.

As we ventured out, I couldn't believe the wonder below us. We saw turtles, schools of different fish, and vibrant coral reefs that seemed to stretch for miles. A bit further out, there was an inflatable trampoline and playground, and although I had no intent on doing that, I did want to see how far we swam. I was having such a great time, and the water was so clear that I could still see the bottom of the ocean. This led me to believe that we hadn't gone that far. I soon found out I was wrong. When I lifted my head out of the water, I saw that we were only a few feet away from our cruise ship. This created sheer panic for me! All I could think was that for the boat to dock, the water had to be deep; therefore, we were definitely in some deep water, and that wasn't for me! I lost my composure and calmness had left my body. I never eased my grip on my cousin. She was amazing and did wonderfully with me. She reassured me I was safe and that she would get me back to land. I never fully recovered to my relaxed state but trusted her to lead the way to get me back to shore. So, when I decided to go snorkeling in Barbados, several years later, I realized this was a big deal, especially because my confidence was shot after my stroke. Worse, my confidence was shot after a near-drowning accident about a year and a half ago.

In October of 2019, I was in Costa Rica to celebrate a dear friend's birthday, someone who has become a sister to me. While in Costa Rica, I wanted to see if I was able to swim after having my strokes. I went to the five-foot side of the pool to see what I could do. I started to go under, took my feet off the floor of the pool, and submerged under the water. When I tried to come up, I completely lost it. The nightmare I feared was true. Due to my stroke, I lost the trust I gained from swimming lessons. I believe that when I regained my short-term memory, part of my memory wasn't restored.

In Barbados, I had the chance to be near such beautiful water again, and I just had to try snorkeling again. I found a guy that gave me an amazing deal. When I went on the boat, I let the driver know I wanted to do it, but I was scared. He assured me he would take care of me and help me snorkel. We got to our first stop to explore the turtles and other ocean life. With much hesitation, I got in the water with the driver by my side. We set out to enjoy the wonderful sea life, and it felt good. We went out for about 15 minutes and did some exploring. As we worked our way back to the boat, my fear seemed to have subsided. Me and the other visitors got in the boat and headed to see the sunken ship. When we got to the ship, I was determined to do it by myself. I got into the water, and at that moment realized this was really happening. Initially, I held on the side of the boat with one hand and started floating. I still was a little nervous about letting go, but I did it – I let go of the boat. I was in the ocean, snorkeling all by myself, and loving it. I swam around and looked at all the life below me – turtles, stingrays, and multi-colored fish – everything was just beautiful. That was the moment I realized how much courage I had and knew I could and would take on more things I normally wouldn't pursue.

Everyone has a definition of "living my best life." At the end of the day, living life to the fullest with what you have is key. We all are granted the same 24 hours and have the ability to make the most out of those precious hours. I've had many obstacles, challenges, and setbacks, but through it all, I remain determined to make this thing called life count. Each day of my life, I am "Purposed to *Live*."

Full Circle

After sharing a small glimpse into my life, I set forth various challenges to you:

Become an Overcomer

"To realize your greatest strengths, you must first overcome your greatest weakness."
Matshona Dhliwayo

Whether an emotional, physical, mental, or spiritual battle affects you from the past or in the present day, I encourage you to fight to overcome. Make every effort to defeat, overcome, and heal. Know that you deserve to win. You don't have to let anything that has happened define you. Everyone has faced battles in life. Damage comes from so many places – the world, enemies, friends, and even family – but you must fight and come out on top with scars and all. Battle wounds don't negate defeat; they represent a fight that took place, and you came out alive, proving you are capable of being a victor.

Change Your Mindset

"Once your mindset changes, everything on the outside will change along with it."

Steve Maraboli

When looking at your situation and circumstances, change your mindset. Don't continue to look at things the same way. Try to allow yourself to see a new perspective. If you're used to saying, "why me," change that language and start saying, "why not me!" This mindset allows you to know you are more than capable of handling whatever comes your way.

It's easy to drown in a negative mindset. Change that mindset and see the bigger picture that can come forth from your situation.

Seek to Live Beyond Limits

"And there were four leprous men at the entering in of the gate: and they said one to another, Why sit here until we die? If we say, We will enter into the city, then the famine is in the city, and we shall die there: and if we sit still here, we die also. Now therefore come, and let us fall unto the host of the Syrians: if they save us alive, we shall live; and if they kill us, we shall but die. And they rose up in the twilight, to go unto the camp of the Syrians: and when they were come to the uttermost part of the camp of Syria, behold, there was no man there."

2 Kings 3:5

You can take your life to new heights by

not allowing yourself to have a ceiling mentality. Start believing like never before. Understand that you can achieve more but must be willing to have faith to endure whatever comes your way in the process.

I grew up in a small town, but that small town was just one piece of me. This town works for a lot of people, and there's nothing wrong with that. However, I knew my life was meant for more than this small town could offer. After I graduated high school, I left my small town. I graduated from college, returned to the small town, and stayed for six months. I couldn't shake the feeling that life was so much more than where I was and a whole big world waiting for me. So, I put forth the effort to get a job that would help me get out of there. After searching, I got that job, left, and never looked back. Whatever you dream of, believe in, and hope for, go forth and get it. Take the leap of faith and go after whatever you desire. Whether you've been talked down to, told you can't, heard you won't amount to anything, convinced yourself you can't, or talked yourself into believing your dreams are impossible, try again and try to live beyond those limits set upon you.

Don't Submit to the Diagnosis

"But He was wounded for our transgressions, He was bruised for our iniquities; The chastisement for our peace was upon Him, And by His stripes we are healed."
Isaiah 53:5

Be thankful for modern science and technological advancements. However, whatever the diagnosis, take the information and fight. The diagnosis given is the information needed to know what you are praying and fighting for specifically. Any negative news dealing with your well-being can be devastating. You have a choice to accept the news as the absolute truth for your life, or you can take the information and believe for a greater outcome. I challenge you to believe beyond what you see, hear, and feel, and set your mind to a level of faith where you're free to believe in greater things for your life. Never let the diagnosis define you. Take the diagnosis and believe you can defeat it.

***

Never be afraid to push yourself to achieve your goals. Remember – you can change your narrative! Not a day goes by that I don't think about those few seconds that changed my life. I could allow myself to succumb to constantly thinking that the next moment could be my last moment. Instead, I have chosen to live each moment to the fullest and make it count. I have my eyes set on living and enjoying all I can while I'm here. So, when I'm at my 80th birthday party, and I blow out those candles, I want to remember all the good times, and when I'm blessed to see 90 years old, I'm going to sit in my rocking chair and look back at the memories I created on this journey called life. With tears in my eyes and a smile on my face, I will simply look up to Heaven and say, "Thank You, Lord, for every way you've made!"

www.ingramcontent.com/pod-product-compliance
Lightning Source LLC
Chambersburg PA
CBHW031550040426
42452CB00006B/258